**Great Works** Instructional Guide for **Literature**

The Great Kapok Tree

A guide for the book by Lynne Cherry
Great Works Author: Brenda Van Dixhorn

SHELL EDUCATION

Image Credits

Shutterstock (cover; pages 1, 11–12, 22, 40, 50, 56, 70); Timothy J. Bradley (pages 29, 62–64)

Standards

© 2007 Teachers of English to Speakers of Other Languages, Inc. (TESOL)
© 2007 Board of Regents of the University of Wisconsin System. World-Class Instructional Design and Assessment (WIDA)
© Copyright 2010. National Governors Association Center for Best Practices and Council of Chief State School Officers. All rights reserved.

Shell Education

5301 Oceanus Drive
Huntington Beach, CA 92649-1030
http://www.shelleducation.com
ISBN 978-1-4258-8958-6
© 2015 Shell Educational Publishing, Inc.

Table of Contents

How to Use This Literature Guide

Today's standards demand rigor and relevance in the reading of complex texts. The units in this series guide teachers in a rich and deep exploration of worthwhile works of literature for classroom study. The most rigorous instruction can also be interesting and engaging!

Many current strategies for effective literacy instruction have been incorporated into these instructional guides for literature. Throughout the units, text-dependent questions are used to determine comprehension of the book as well as student interpretation of the vocabulary words. The books chosen for the series are complex and are exemplars of carefully crafted works of literature. Close reading is used throughout the units to guide students toward revisiting the text and using textual evidence to respond to prompts orally and in writing. Students must analyze the story elements in multiple assignments for each section of the book. All of these strategies work together to rigorously guide students through their study of literature.

The next few pages describe how to use this guide for a purposeful and meaningful literature study. Each section of this guide is set up in the same way to make it easier for you to implement the instruction in your classroom.

Theme Thoughts

The great works of literature used throughout this series have important themes that have been relevant to people for many years. Many of the themes will be discussed during the various sections of this instructional guide. However, it would also benefit students to have independent time to think about the key themes of the book.

Before students begin reading, have them complete the *Pre-Reading Theme Thoughts* (page 14). This graphic organizer will allow students to think about the themes outside the context of the story. They'll have the opportunity to evaluate statements based on important themes and defend their opinions. Be sure to keep students' papers for comparison to the *Post-Reading Theme Thoughts* (page 60). This graphic organizer is similar to the pre-reading activity. However, this time, students will be answering the questions from the point of view of one of the characters in the book. They have to think about how the character would feel about each statement and defend their thoughts. To conclude the activity, have students compare what they thought about the themes before they read the book to what the characters discovered during the story.

How to Use This Literature Guide (cont.)

Vocabulary

Each teacher reference vocabulary overview page has definitions and sentences about how key vocabulary words are used in the section. These words should be introduced and discussed with students. Students will use these words in different activities throughout the book.

On some of the vocabulary student pages, students are asked to answer text-related questions about vocabulary words from the sections. The following question stems will help you create your own vocabulary questions if you'd like to extend the discussion.

- How does this word describe _____'s character?
- How does this word connect to the problem in this story?
- How does this word help you understand the setting?
- Tell me how this word connects to the main idea of this story.
- What visual pictures does this word bring to your mind?
- Why do you think the author used this word?

At times, you may find that more work with the words will help students understand their meanings and importance. These quick vocabulary activities are a good way to further study the words.

- Students can play vocabulary concentration. Make one set of cards that has the words on them and another set with the definitions. Then, have students lay them out on the table and play concentration. The goal of the game is to match vocabulary words with their definitions. For early readers or English language learners, the two sets of cards could be the words and pictures of the words.

- Students can create word journal entries about the words. Students choose words they think are important and then describe why they think each word is important within the book. Early readers or English language learners could instead draw pictures about the words in a journal.

- Students can create puppets and use them to act out the vocabulary words from the stories. Students may also enjoy telling their own character-driven stories using vocabulary words from the original stories.

How to Use This Literature Guide (cont.)

Analyzing the Literature

After you have read each section with students, hold a small-group or whole-class discussion. Provided on the teacher reference page for each section are leveled questions. The questions are written at two levels of complexity to allow you to decide which questions best meet the needs of your students. The Level 1 questions are typically less abstract than the Level 2 questions. These questions are focused on the various story elements, such as character, setting, and plot. Be sure to add further questions as your students discuss what they've read. For each question, a few key points are provided for your reference as you discuss the book with students.

Reader Response

In today's classrooms, there are often great readers who are below average writers. So much time and energy is spent in classrooms getting students to read on grade level that little time is left to focus on writing skills. To help teachers include more writing in their daily literacy instruction, each section of this guide has a literature-based reader response prompt. Each of the three genres of writing is used in the reader responses within this guide: narrative, informative/explanatory, and opinion. Before students write, you may want to allow them time to draw pictures related to the topic. Book-themed writing paper is provided on page 70 if your students need more space to write.

Guided Close Reading

Within each section of this guide, it is suggested that you closely reread a portion of the text with your students. No page numbers are given because some versions of the book do not have page numbers. The sections to be reread are described by location. After rereading the section, there are a few text-dependent questions to be answered by students.

Working space has been provided to help students prepare for the group discussion. They should record their thoughts and ideas on the activity page and refer to it during your discussion. Rather than just taking notes, you may want to require students to write complete responses to the questions before discussing them with you.

Encourage students to read one question at a time and then go back to the text and discover the answer. Work with students to ensure that they use the text to determine their answers rather than making unsupported inferences. Suggested answers are provided in the answer key.

How to Use This Literature Guide (cont.)

Guided Close Reading (cont.)

The generic open-ended stems below can be used to write your own text-dependent questions if you would like to give students more practice.

- What words in the story support . . . ?
- What text helps you understand . . . ?
- Use the book to tell why _____ happens.
- Based on the events in the story, . . . ?
- Show me the part in the text that supports . . . .
- Use the text to tell why . . . .

Making Connections

The activities in this section help students make cross-curricular connections to mathematics, science, social studies, fine arts, or other curricular areas. These activities require higher-order thinking skills from students but also allow for creative thinking.

Language Learning

A special section has been set aside to connect the literature to language conventions. Through these activities, students will have opportunities to practice the conventions of standard English grammar, usage, capitalization, and punctuation.

Story Elements

It is important to spend time discussing what the common story elements are in literature. Understanding the characters, setting, plot, and theme can increase students' comprehension and appreciation of the story. If teachers begin discussing these elements in early childhood, students will more likely internalize the concepts and look for the elements in their independent reading. Another very important reason for focusing on the story elements is that students will be better writers if they think about how the stories they read are constructed.

In the story elements activities, students are asked to create work related to the characters, setting, or plot. Consider having students complete only one of these activities. If you give students a choice on this assignment, each student can decide to complete the activity that most appeals to him or her. Different intelligences are used so that the activities are diverse and interesting to all students.

How to Use This Literature Guide (cont.)

Culminating Activity

At the end of this instructional guide is a creative culminating activity that allows students the opportunity to share what they've learned from reading the book. This activity is open ended so that students can push themselves to create their own great works within your language arts classroom.

Comprehension Assessment

The questions in this section require students to think about the book they've read as well as the words that were used in the book. Some questions are tied to quotations from the book to engage students and require them to think about the text as they answer the questions.

Response to Literature

Finally, students are asked to respond to the literature by drawing pictures and writing about the characters and stories. A suggested rubric is provided for teacher reference.

Correlation to the Standards

Shell Education is committed to producing educational materials that are research and standards based. As part of this effort, we have correlated all of our products to the academic standards of all 50 states, the District of Columbia, the Department of Defense Dependents Schools, and all Canadian provinces.

Purpose and Intent of Standards

Standards are designed to focus instruction and guide adoption of curricula. Standards are statements that describe the criteria necessary for students to meet specific academic goals. They define the knowledge, skills, and content students should acquire at each level. Standards are also used to develop standardized tests to evaluate students' academic progress. Teachers are required to demonstrate how their lessons meet standards. Standards are used in the development of all of our products, so educators can be assured they meet high academic standards.

How to Find Standards Correlations

To print a customized correlation report of this product for your state, visit our website at http://www.shelleducation.com and follow the online directions. If you require assistance in printing correlation reports, please contact our Customer Service Department at 1-877-777-3450.

Correlation to the Standards (cont.)

Standards Correlation Chart

The lessons in this book were written to support the Common Core College and Career Readiness Anchor Standards. The following chart indicates which lessons address the anchor standards.

Common Core College and Career Readiness Anchor Standard	Section
CCSS.ELA-Literacy.CCRA.R.1—Read closely to determine what the text says explicitly and to make logical inferences from it; cite specific textual evidence when writing or speaking to support conclusions drawn from the text.	Analyzing the Literature Sections 1–5; Guided Close Reading Sections 1–5; Story Elements Sections 2–5; Making Connections Section 1; Culminating Activity
CCSS.ELA-Literacy.CCRA.R.2—Determine central ideas or themes of a text and analyze their development; summarize the key supporting details and ideas.	Guided Close Reading Sections 1–5; Story Elements Sections 1, 4–5; Making Connections Section 5; Culminating Activity
CCSS.ELA-Literacy.CCRA.R.3—Analyze how and why individuals, events, or ideas develop and interact over the course of a text.	Analyzing the Literature Sections 1–5; Making Connections Section 3; Story Elements Sections 1, 3–5
CCSS.ELA-Literacy.CCRA.R.4—Interpret words and phrases as they are used in a text, including determining technical, connotative, and figurative meanings, and analyze how specific word choices shape meaning or tone.	Vocabulary Sections 1–5; Language Learning Section 3
CCSS.ELA-Literacy.CCRA.R.6—Assess how point of view or purpose shapes the content and style of a text.	Guided Close Reading Sections 1–5; Story Elements Section 2
CCSS.ELA-Literacy.CCRA.W.1—Write arguments to support claims in an analysis of substantive topics or texts using valid reasoning and relevant and sufficient evidence.	Reader Response Sections 3, 5
CCSS.ELA-Literacy.CCRA.W.2—Write informative/ explanatory texts to examine and convey complex ideas and information clearly and accurately through the effective selection, organization, and analysis of content.	Reader Response Section 1
CCSS.ELA-Literacy.CCRA.W.3—Write narratives to develop real or imagined experiences or events using effective technique, well-chosen details and well-structured event sequences.	Story Elements Sections 1, 4; Reader Response Sections 2, 4
CCSS.ELA-Literacy.CCRA.W.4—Produce clear and coherent writing in which the development, organization, and style are appropriate to task, purpose, and audience.	Reader Response Sections 1–5; Story Elements Section 1

Common Core College and Career Readiness Anchor Standard	Section
CCSS.ELA-Literacy.CCRA.W.7—Conduct short as well as more sustained research projects based on focused questions, demonstrating understanding of the subject under investigation.	Making Connections Section 4
CCSS.ELA-Literacy.CCRA.L.1—Demonstrate command of the conventions of standard English grammar and usage when writing or speaking.	Vocabulary Section 1; Language Learning Sections 1–5
CCSS.ELA-Literacy.CCRA.L.2—Demonstrate command of the conventions of standard English capitalization, punctuation, and spelling when writing.	Post-Reading Response to Literature
CCSS.ELA-Literacy.CCRA.L.4—Determine or clarify the meaning of unknown and multiple-meaning words and phrases by using context clues, analyzing meaningful word parts, and consulting general and specialized reference materials, as appropriate.	Vocabulary Sections 1–5
CCSS.ELA-Literacy.CCRA.L.5—Demonstrate understanding of figurative language, word relationships, and nuances in word meanings.	Language Learning Sections 1, 5; Story Elements Section 4
CCSS.ELA-Literacy.CCRA.L.6—Acquire and use accurately a range of general academic and domain-specific words and phrases sufficient for reading, writing, speaking, and listening at the college and career readiness level; demonstrate independence in gathering vocabulary knowledge when encountering an unknown term important to comprehension or expression.	Vocabulary Sections 1–5

TESOL and WIDA Standards

The lessons in this book promote English language development for English language learners. The following TESOL and WIDA English Language Development Standards are addressed through the activities in this book:

- **Standard 1:** English language learners communicate for social and instructional purposes within the school setting.

- **Standard 2:** English language learners communicate information, ideas and concepts necessary for academic success in the content area of language arts.

About the Author—Lynne Cherry

Lynne Cherry cares deeply about the earth and has spent much of her career encouraging young readers to do their part to care for our world. Cherry has written and/or illustrated more than 30 books for children. The message in many of her books is that people, especially children, can make the world a better place for all its inhabitants.

Cherry was born in Philadelphia, Pennsylvania, in 1952. As a young child, she spent time in the woods and fields of Pennsylvania learning to love plants and animals. While in elementary school, Cherry wrote and illustrated her first books. She attended art school and earned a teaching degree at Temple University. Cherry received her master's degree in history from Yale University. She has served as an artist in residence at many institutions, including the Smithsonian, Princeton University, and the Woods Hole Oceanographic Institution.

Along with writing and illustrating, Cherry is well known for filmmaking. She has directed and produced seven short movies that tell stories of children who have made differences in the environment. Cherry believes that everyone can take steps to improve our planet.

Lynne Cherry has won numerous awards for her books. A complete listing of Cherry's books and awards, links to interviews with Cherry, ways to make a difference, and more can be found at her website: **http://members.authorsguild.net/lynnecherry/index.htm**.

Possible Texts for Text Comparisons

The theme of improving our planet runs through all of Lynne Cherry's books. *A River Ran Wild: An Environmental History; How Groundhog's Garden Grew; The Armadillo from Amarillo; The Sea, the Storm, and the Mangrove Tangle;* and *The Shaman's Apprentice: A Tale of the Amazon Rain Forest* provide messages similar to those found in *The Great Kapok Tree.*

Book Summary of *The Great Kapok Tree*

A young man is instructed to chop down a Kapok tree in the Amazon Rain Forest. After working for a time, he becomes tired, sits down, and falls asleep. Residents of the rain forest come to the young man while he sleeps, each sharing with him the importance of the tree. The young man is visited by many animals and a native child whose lives would change dramatically if the tree were removed. Upon awakening, the young man ponders the messages he heard while asleep, recognizes the importance of the tree, drops his ax, and leaves the forest.

Cross-Curricular Connection

This book can enhance science units on animals, rain forests, and protecting the environment.

Possible Texts for Text Sets

- Aloian, Molly and Bobbie Kalman. *A Rainforest Habitat*. National Geographic School Pub, 2010.
- Brett, Jan. *The Umbrella*. Putnam Juvenile, 2004.
- Carle, Eric. *"Slowly, Slowly, Slowly," said the Sloth*. Puffin, 2007.
- Fredericks, Anthony D. *A is for Anaconda: A Rain Forest Alphabet*. Sleeping Bear Press, 2009.
- Mitchell, Susan K. *The Rainforest Grew All Around*. Sylvan Dell Publishing, 2007.
- Seuss, Dr. *The Lorax*. Random House Books for Young Readers, 1971.

How to Read the Book

Each section of this instructional guide contains lessons and activities to help students gain an understanding of the story and related vocabulary in a variety of ways. A summary of each section is given below to be a guide as you share this book with your class.

Section 1: Entering the Rain Forest

This section begins with the preface of the book. The section ends after the first two pages of text when the man falls asleep. The rain forest is described, and the reader is introduced to the man charged with cutting down the great Kapok tree.

Section 2: Four Groups Visit

Animals visit the sleeping man and explain the importance of the tree. Read over the pages where the boa constrictor, bee, monkeys, and birds visit the man.

Note: The Making Connections activity in this section asks students to create a family tree. A tree has been provided with spots for parents and grandparents. Due to the many different family situations in each classroom, you may find that providing just a tree outline may be better for your students. Match your knowledge of your students with this activity, and encourage them to create tree diagrams that reflect their families.

Section 3: Five More Groups Visit

More animals try to convince the sleeping man that the Kapok tree needs to remain in the forest. Read over the pages where the tree frog, jaguar, tree porcupines, anteaters, and a three-toed sloth implore the man to leave the tree alone.

Section 4: A Child's Visit

The Yanomamo tribe child visits just before the man awakens. Upon awakening, the man sees the tree, animals, and forest with a new understanding. The man's new point of view is described.

Section 5: Leaving the Forest

The man picks up his ax and swings it to strike the tree. Instead, however, he decides to walk out of the rain forest without cutting down the Kapok tree. Some editions of the book also include a letter to the reader from Lynne Cherry.

Name _____ Date _____

Pre-Reading Theme Thoughts

Directions: Draw a picture of a happy face or a sad face. Your face should show how you feel about each statement. Then, use words to say what you think about each statement.

Statement	How Do You Feel? 😊 ☹	Explain Your Answer
You should follow directions without thinking of the consequences.		
It is all right to cut down a tree in a forest.		
People can change their minds while they sleep.		
One person can make a difference in the world.		

Vocabulary Overview

Key words and phrases from this section are provided below with definitions and sentences about how the words are used in the story. Introduce and discuss these important vocabulary words with students. If you think these words or other words in the story warrant more time devoted to them, there are suggestions in the introduction for other vocabulary activities (page 5).

Word or Phrase	Definition	Sentence about Text
Amazon Rain Forest (preface)	a forest with heavy rainfall located in South America	This story takes place in the **Amazon Rain Forest**.
canopy (preface)	a roof-like covering	In a rain forest, the tops of trees are called the **canopy**.
understory (preface)	plants and trees that grow under the canopy of a forest	The **understory** is the lower level of the rain forest.
Kapok tree (preface)	a large tree that grows in tropical places	Many animals make their homes in the **Kapok tree**.
emerges (preface)	comes into view	The Kapok tree is so tall, it **emerges** above the canopy of the rain forest.
community (preface)	a group living in a particular area	The rain forest is home to a large **community** of animals.
moments	a short amount of time	The animals make noises **moments** before the men enter the rain forest.
squawking	a sudden, loud cry	You might hear **squawking** birds in the rain forest.
howling	an animal's loud cry	The noise monkeys make is called **howling**.
lulled	calmed or made someone feel relaxed	The sounds of the forest **lull** the man to sleep.

Name _____ Date _____

Vocabulary Activity

Directions: Draw lines to complete the sentences.

Sentence Beginnings	Sentence Endings

The Great Kapok Tree is the story of a **community**

Squawking and **howling** sounds are made

The great Kapok tree is so tall

The **canopy** is a high and sunny place that

The heat and sounds of the rain forest

looks like it touches the sky.

it **emerges** above the other trees in the forest.

lull the man to sleep.

of animals that live in a tree.

by the birds and monkeys in the forest.

Directions: Answer this question.

1. What things would you see in the **understory** of a rainforest?

_____

_____

Analyzing the Literature

Provided here are discussion questions you can use in small groups, with the whole class, or for written assignments. Each question is written at two levels so that you can choose the right question for each group of students. For each question, a few key points are provided for your reference as you discuss the book with students.

Story Element	Level 1	Level 2	Key Discussion Points
Setting	Using what you learned in the preface of the book, describe the Amazon Rain Forest.	What similarities and differences are there between the Amazon Rain Forest and where you live?	The book describes the rain forest as being hot and a good climate in which plants can grow. There are many layers of plants. The upper layer is the canopy, and that layer has lots of exposure to sunlight. The bottom layer is the understory and is much darker. There are many animals that live in the rain forest. Discuss characteristics of where you live to find similarities and differences.
Character	Name some animals that live in the rain forest.	Why do the animals make their homes in the different parts of the rain forest?	The book lists parrots, monkeys, snakes, and jaguars as being inhabitants of the rain forest. Animals that like the light, such as birds and monkeys, live in the canopy. Animals that like to live in darkness, such as snakes and jaguars, live in the understory.
Setting	What is the rain forest like before the men walk in?	Why do you think the animals become silent after the men enter the rain forest?	Before the men enter the forest, the animals are making sounds. Monkeys are howling and birds are squawking. As the men enter, all the animals become silent. The animals watch and wait to see what the men will do.
Plot	Why do the two men walk into the rain forest?	What happens to the smaller man in the rain forest?	Two men walk into the rain forest. "The larger man" comes to give instructions, and the second man comes to work. As he begins the job of chopping down the tree, the smaller man becomes tired and eventually falls asleep.

Name _____ Date _____

Reader Response

Think

You meet many animals in *The Great Kapok Tree*. Think about your favorite animal. It may live in the wild, a zoo, or even in your house.

Informative/Explanatory Writing Prompt

Describe your favorite animal. Tell where it lives, what it does, and what it eats. Provide as much interesting information about your favorite animal as you can.

_____

_____

_____

_____

_____

_____

_____

_____

_____

Guided Close Reading

Closely reread the first section of the book. Start with the preface and read the first two pages of text in the story.

Directions: Think about these questions. In the space below, write ideas or draw pictures as you think. Be ready to share your answers.

---

❶ What words in the book describe how it feels to be in the Amazon Rain Forest?

---

❷ Use the text to tell how the animals feel about the men who enter the forest.

---

❸ Which of the two men is in charge? Use the text to tell how you know this.

Name _____ Date _____

Making Connections-A Rain Forest

Directions: The book talks about the layers of a rain forest and the plants and animals that live in those layers. Draw a picture of a rain forest below. Label the canopy and understory. Place at least three animals in each layer of your rain forest. Write the animal names beside their pictures. You may want to look online or in other rain forest books to help find information for your drawings.

Name _____ Date _____

Language Learning–Onomatopoeia

Directions: Work with a partner to find at least two onomatopoeia words in the story. Write each word, draw a picture that illustrates the word, and write a sentence using each word.

Language Hints!

- Onomatopoeia words remind you of sounds.

- The words *whack* and *chop* are examples from the story.

Onomatopoeia #1: _____

\
\
\
\

_____

_____

Onomatopoeia #2: _____

\
\
\
\

_____

_____

Name _____ Date _____

Story Elements-Plot

Directions: Two men enter the rain forest. On the lines below, write what you think the men are talking about from the time they enter the rain forest until the larger man leaves. Remember to use quotation marks to show when someone is speaking.

_____

_____

_____

_____

_____

_____

_____

_____

_____

_____

_____

_____

Story Elements–Setting

Directions: This story is set in a rain forest and is about a community of animals. In an ocean, the community of animals might include whales, sharks, fish, jellyfish, lobsters, and sea stars. If the setting were a construction site, the community might include truck drivers, builders, electricians, plumbers, and architects. Select two other possible settings for a story. List the settings and make lists of who would be part of the community in each setting.

Setting 1

Community Members

Setting 2

Community Members

#40105—Instructional Guide: The Great Kapok Tree

Vocabulary Overview

Key words and phrases from this section are provided below with definitions and sentences about how the words are used in the story. Introduce and discuss these important vocabulary words with students. If you think these words or other words in the story warrant more time devoted to them, there are suggestions in the introduction for other vocabulary activities (page 5).

Word	Definition	Sentence about Text
slithered	moved silently in a sideways motion	The snake **slithers** down the Kapok tree.
gash	a deep cut	The man's ax leaves a **gash** in the trunk of the Kapok tree.
hissed	a sharp sound that showed disapproval	The snake is not happy when he **hisses** in the man's ear.
miracles	marvelous events	The snake tells the man that the tree is a tree of **miracles**.
generations	groups of people who live at the same time	Your classmates are part of your **generation**.
ancestors	relatives who came before someone	**Ancestors** can be your parents, grandparents, and great-grandparents.
pollinate	transfer of pollen from one plant to another	A bee works to **pollinate** plants and flowers.
depend	to rely on someone or something	Pets **depend** on their owners to provide food and shelter.
troupe	a collection of people or animals	The **troupe** of monkeys speaks to the man.
wither	shrivel up or shrink	Plants will **wither** if not cared for properly.
underbrush	smaller plants growing under larger trees in a forest	Cutting down the Kapok tree will hurt the **underbrush**, as well.
smoldering	a fire that is smoking but not in flame	After a forest fire, only **smoldering** ruins are left.

Vocabulary Activity

Directions: Choose at least three words from the story. Draw a picture that shows what these words mean. Label your picture.

Words from the Story

slithered	underbrush	hissed	miracles
pollinate	depend	troupe	wither
generations	ancestors	gash	smoldering

Directions: Answer this question.

1. What would cause a plant in the rain forest to **wither**?

_____

Analyzing the Literature

Provided here are discussion questions you can use in small groups, with the whole class, or for written assignments. Each question is written at two levels so that you can choose the right question for each group of students. For each question, a few key points are provided for your reference as you discuss the book with students.

Story Element	Level 1	Level 2	Key Discussion Points
Plot	What animals come to give the man a message in this section?	What is the theme of the message that the animals bring to the sleeping man?	A boa constrictor, bee, troupe of monkeys, and birds (toucan, macaw, and cock-of-the-rock) all speak to the man. They try to convince the man not to cut down the Kapok tree.
Setting	How do the animals feel about the great Kapok tree?	Why is the great Kapok tree so important to these animals?	The animals feel strongly that the great Kapok tree should remain where it is. The tree is their home and was the home of their ancestors. It helps hold the forest in place, and cutting down trees ruins the rain forest.
Character	How many animals do you think come to visit the man in this section of the story?	Describe the animals that speak to the man.	There is not an exact number of visiting animals because we are not told how many are in the troupe of monkeys. It is safe to assume more than six (boa constrictor, bee, monkeys, toucan, macaw, and cock-of-the-rock) come with messages. Physical traits (as seen in the illustrations) or character traits (concerned, worried, upset, unhappy, or scared) can be discussed when describing the animals.
Plot	What is the monkeys' greatest concern?	Explain the series of events the monkeys believe will lead to the forest becoming a desert.	The monkeys are afraid that once people chop down one tree, they will not hesitate to cut down more and more. As the trees are removed, their roots will wither and die, leaving the soil to wash away in heavy rains. As that happens, the forest will become a desert.

Reader Response

Think

The bee tells the sleeping man that living things depend on each other. Think about when you have had to depend or rely on someone.

Narrative Writing Prompt

Write about a time in your life when you had to depend on someone to help you complete a task or accomplish a goal. What did you want to do, and how did the other person help you?

_____

_____

_____

_____

_____

_____

_____

_____

_____

_____

Name _____ Date _____

Guided Close Reading

Closely reread the pages with the first four groups of visiting animals. You should read about the boa constrictor, bee, troupe of monkeys, and the birds.

Directions: Think about these questions. In the space below, write ideas or draw pictures as you think. Be ready to share your answers.

❶ What details explain how all living things depend on each other?

❷ What words do the animals use to let the man know he should not cut down the Kapok tree?

❸ What do you think it means when the boa constrictor hisses: "Senhor, this tree is a tree of miracles"?

Making Connections–Family Tree

Directions: The boa constrictor says that generations of his ancestors have lived in the Kapok tree. A family tree is one way of displaying family members from different generations. Draw pictures and name your family members on the tree below.

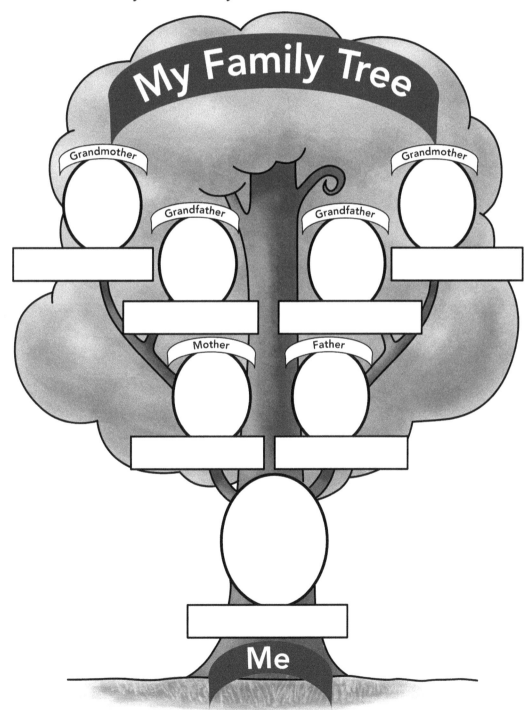

Name _____ Date _____

Language Learning–Interesting Verbs

Directions: The author of *The Great Kapok Tree* uses interesting verbs to show the actions of the animals in the story. Make a list of the interesting ways each animal listed below moves and communicates.

Language Hints!

- Verbs are words that show action.

- Verbs show what happens in a sentence.

Animal	Verbs
boa constrictor	
bee	
troupe of monkeys	
toucan, macaw, and cock-of-the-rock	

Directions: Write a sentence using at least two interesting verbs from the book.

_____

_____

Story Elements-Character

Directions: Chose an animal from this section and draw a picture to show what it looks like. You may look in the book or at an online resource to help with your drawing.

Animals in this Section

boa constrictor	bee	troupe of monkeys
toucan	macaw	cock-of-the-rock

Directions: Write at least two sentences describing the animal you drew.

_____

_____

_____

#40105—Instructional Guide: The Great Kapok Tree

Story Elements-Setting

Directions: The Kapok tree is of great importance to the animals that live in it. Pretend that you are one of the animals from the Kapok tree. Write a letter telling the tree why it is so important to you. Remember to include the elements of a friendly letter when you write.

Date: _____

Greeting: _____ ,

_____

_____

_____

_____

_____

_____

_____

_____

Closing: _____ ,

Signature: _____

Vocabulary Overview

Key words and phrases from this section are provided below with definitions and sentences about how the words are used in the story. Introduce and discuss these important vocabulary words with students. If you think these words or other words in the story warrant more time devoted to them, there are suggestions in the introduction for other vocabulary activities (page 5).

Word or Phrase	Definition	Sentence about Text
piped	made a shrill cry	The tree frog **pipes** in the man's ear.
ruined	destroyed	The animals are afraid the forest will be **ruined**.
dappled	marks or spots of color	The jaguar has a **dappled** coat.
padded	moved about quietly on foot	The **padded** steps of the jaguar are silent.
oxygen	the air we breathe	Animals and people in the rain forest depend on **oxygen** to stay alive.
produce	to make or create	Trees **produce** the oxygen we breathe.
clinging	holding on to something tightly	The baby anteaters are **clinging** to their mothers' backs.
future	the time that will come	The animals are worried about the **future** of the rain forest.
plodding	walking at a very slow pace	The sloth made slow, **plodding** steps to reach the man.
feast your eyes	look at with enjoyment	**Feast your eyes** on the beauty of the rain forest.

Vocabulary Activity

Directions: Each of these sentences contains a word from the story. Cut apart these sentence strips. Put the sentences in order. Use the story to help you.

The jaguar's spotted coat blends into the **dappled** light and shadows of the understory.

The anteaters climb down the tree with their babies **clinging** to them.

The tree porcupines ask the man if he knows what trees **produce**.

The tree frog tells the man that a **ruined** rain forest means **ruined** lives.

The three-toed sloth points out that if the rain forest is destroyed, they won't have anything to **feast their eyes** on.

The anteater says, "Senhor, you are chopping down this tree with no thought for the **future**."

Analyzing the Literature

Provided here are discussion questions you can use in small groups, with the whole class, or for written assignments. Each question is written at two levels so that you can choose the right question for each group of students. For each question, a few key points are provided for your reference as you discuss the book with students.

Story Element	Level 1	Level 2	Key Discussion Points
Plot	What does the tree frog tell the man will happen if he chops down the tree?	What does the tree frog mean when he says, "A ruined forest means ruined lives"?	The tree frog tells the man that many will be left homeless if he chops down the Kapok tree. Lives will be ruined because animals will not have places to live. If the forest is destroyed, there will be no shelter for any of the animals and all of the plants that grow there will be destroyed.
Character	Describe the jaguar.	What keeps the jaguar from being noticed?	The jaguar has been sleeping. His coat is spotted. The sun shines unevenly through the canopy of the rain forest leaving the understory dappled with shadows and light. The jaguar's spotted coat blends in and makes him difficult to see.
Setting	What plants are part of the rain forest?	Describe the Kapok tree.	Along with the great Kapok tree, there are smaller trees growing near the ground. The tree frog crawls along the edge of a leaf. Encourage students to look at the illustrations and name other plants they see. The Kapok tree is quite large. A branch in the tree supports a sleeping jaguar, there is room for porcupines to swing from branch to branch, and it takes a sloth most of the story to climb down from the top of the tree.
Plot	What concern do the anteaters share with the man?	Why are the anteaters so concerned about the future?	The anteaters are concerned that if this tree is cut down, more will follow, and someday children will live in a world with no trees. The anteaters approach the man with their own young. Having young children of their own likely causes them to ponder what the world will be like in the future.

Name _____ Date _____

Reader Response

Think

Each animal that speaks to the man presents a different reason for not cutting down the Kapok tree. Think about the reasons that have been presented for leaving the tree alone. Which reason do you think is the best?

Opinion Writing Prompt

Write about the best reason for not cutting down the great Kapok tree. Describe why you think it is a good reason.

_____

_____

_____

_____

_____

_____

_____

_____

Guided Close Reading

Closely reread the pages with the next five groups of visiting animals. You should read about the tree frog, jaguar, tree porcupines, anteaters, and three-toed sloth.

Directions: Think about these questions. In the space below, write ideas or draw pictures as you think. Be ready to share your answers.

❶ What words describe how the jaguar feels about the Kapok tree being cut down?

❷ Use the text to explain why the Kapok tree is important to the three-toed sloth.

❸ According to the animals, how would cutting down the Kapok tree physically harm the animals?

Name _____ Date _____

Making Connections–Cause and Effect

Directions: The anteaters tell the man that what happens tomorrow depends on what is done today. This is called cause and effect. Think about the situations given. Determine each missing cause or effect, and write it in the appropriate space.

Cause	Effect
Did not complete homework	
	Had a hard time waking up in the morning
	Got a good grade on the math test
Went to the library	
Left the lunch you packed for school at home	

Directions: Write two cause-and-effect situations from the book.

Cause	Effect

Name _____ Date _____

Language Learning–Idioms

Directions: In the book, the sloth asks the man what he would "feast his eyes" on if the rain forests were destroyed. Read each of the idioms. Draw a fun picture showing what it sounds like based on what the words mean. Then think about the message in each idiom, and draw a picture showing what it really means.

Language Hints!

- Idioms are expressions that cannot be understood by just knowing the meanings of the individual words.

- When idioms are used, the reader needs to stop and think about the message.

Idiom: A piece of cake

What does it sound like?	What does it really mean?

Idiom: Hit the books

What does it sound like?	What does it really mean?

Name _____ Date _____

Story Elements–Plot

Directions: Many reasons for not cutting down the tree are presented in the book. Pretend to be a plant or animal living in the rain forest. Write a song about the tree telling why it is so valued and why it should not be cut down.

_____

_____

_____

_____

_____

_____

_____

_____

_____

_____

_____

_____

Story Elements–Character

Directions: The animals in this section of the book are listed below. List the animals in the order they visit the sleeping man. Write a brief description of each animal or describe what worries it.

Animals in this Section

tree porcupines	three-toed sloth	tree frog	anteaters	jaguar

1. _____   _____

    _____

2. _____   _____

    _____

3. _____   _____

    _____

4. _____   _____

    _____

5. _____   _____

    _____

Vocabulary Overview

Key words and phrases from this section are provided below with definitions and sentences about how the words are used in the story. Introduce and discuss these important vocabulary words with students. If you think these words or other words in the story warrant more time devoted to them, there are suggestions in the introduction for other vocabulary activities (page 5).

Word or Phrase	Definition	Sentence about Text
murmur	a quiet sound	The child's voice sounds like a **murmur** in the sleeping man's ear.
new eyes	to see with a different perspective	When the man awakens he should look at the forest with **new eyes**.
depend	to have confidence in someone or something	Many plants and animals **depend** on the great Kapok tree.
wondrous	something that is amazing	The animals of the rain forest are **wondrous**.
rare	something that does not occur often	There are many **rare** plants and animals in the rain forest.
streaming	an ongoing trail of light	The sunlight is **streaming** through the trees.
amidst	surrounded by	The man sleeps **amidst** the forest plants and animals.
dangle	hang or swing	Some plants **dangle** in the breeze.
suspended	to look like something is hanging or floating	Many plants hang **suspended** from the tree branches.
fragrant	having a pleasant smell	The man smells the **fragrant** flowers.

Vocabulary Activity

Directions: Complete each sentence below. Use one of the words listed.

Words from the Story

murmurs	wondrous	rare
amidst	dangle	fragrant

1. The flowers in the rain forest release

   a(n) _____ scent.

2. The man realizes that the animals of the forest are

   _____ and _____.

3. The child _____ his request in

   the man's ear.

4. Sunlight glows like jewels _____ the dark

   colors of the forest.

Directions: Answer this question.

5. What does it mean to see something with **new eyes**?

   _____

   _____

Analyzing the Literature

Provided here are discussion questions you can use in small groups, with the whole class, or for written assignments. Each question is written at two levels so that you can choose the right question for each group of students. For each question, a few key points are provided for your reference as you discuss the book with students.

Story Element	Level 1	Level 2	Key Discussion Points
Character	What does the child ask the man to do when he awakes?	What does the child hope the man will do when he awakes?	The child asks the man to look at the rain forest and all the animals with new eyes. This request shows that the child hopes the man will see the beauty and importance of the forest and decide not to cut down the Kapok tree.
Setting	What does the man see when he awakes?	What might the man hear, feel, and smell when he awakes?	The man sees the rain forest, the native child, and all the animals. He may hear a breeze, but he hears no animal sounds as the book says they are silent. He feels a steamy mist, and he may feel plants and animals as they brush against him. He smells the fragrant plants and possibly some animals.
Plot	What are the animals doing?	Why are the creatures of the forest silent?	The animals are not making any noises at this point. The animals have given their messages to the man and are now quiet, giving him time to think and reflect on what they said.
Character	What words could describe how the man feels when he awakes?	What do you think is going through the man's mind as he awakes?	The man is likely surprised, startled, and maybe scared as he sees all the animals surrounding him. He is probably thinking of what the animals told him and of the beauty of the rain forest.

Reader Response

Think

In this story, the man has an amazing experience when he is asleep. Think about a fantastic dream you have had. How did you feel when you woke up from your dream?

Narrative Writing Prompt

Write about one of your dreams. Give details about what happened in the dream. Explain how the dream made you feel. Describe what you did because of your dream.

_____

_____

_____

_____

_____

_____

_____

_____

_____

Name _____ Date _____

Guided Close Reading

Closely reread the section when the child visits the sleeping man. Begin with the page where the child kneels over the sleeping man, and continue through the page that describes the man looking around and hearing no sounds.

Directions: Think about the questions below. In the space below, write ideas or draw pictures as you think. Be ready to share your answers.

❶ Use the text to describe the child's attitude in approaching the man.

❷ How do the words and illustrations describe the animals of the rain forest?

❸ What words in the text support the idea that the man is beginning to see the forest with *new eyes?*

Making Connections-Places to Live

Directions: The child in this book lives in the rain forest. Draw a picture to answer each question below.

What do you think his house looks like?	What does he do for fun?
What does he see every day?	**What is the weather like?**

Name _____ Date _____

Language Learning–Sensory Writing

Directions: Think of a place to describe. Use the chart to describe what your senses experience in that place. Then, take the information from the chart and write a vivid paragraph about the place.

Language Hints!

- Sensory words tell what you see, smell, feel, taste, and hear.

- Sensory language helps give a more vivid picture of a place.

Place I'm Describing: _____

What I *See*	What I *Smell*
What I *Feel*	What I *Hear*

_____

_____

_____

_____

_____

Story Elements-Setting

Directions: The rain forest is described in great detail in this book. Draw a picture of what you imagine the rain forest looks like. Write a brief description of your drawing on the lines below.

_____

_____

_____

Name _____ Date _____

Story Elements-Character

Directions: The man in the story is having an amazing experience. Pretend you are the man. Think about all you have heard, seen, felt, and smelled. Write a journal entry about your day in the rain forest.

_____

_____

_____

_____

_____

_____

_____

_____

_____

_____

_____

_____

Vocabulary Overview

Key words and phrases from this section are provided below with definitions and sentences about how the words are used in the story. Introduce and discuss these important vocabulary words with the students. If you think these words or other words in the story warrant more time devoted to them, there are suggestions in the introduction for other vocabulary activities (page 5).

Word	Definition	Sentence about Text
strike	to hit something	The man is about to **strike** the tree.
suddenly	happen without warning	He **suddenly** stops swinging the ax.
hesitated	waited or paused before doing something	After he **hesitates**, the man walks out of the forest.
creatures	living things	Many **creatures** live in the rain forest.
planet	a celestial body that moves around a star	Our **planet** is called Earth.
destroyed	ruined or spoiled	We can help keep rain forests from being **destroyed**.
tropical	area near the equator that is warm and humid	This story takes place in a **tropical** rain forest.
temperate	mild; not too warm or cold	There is a **temperate** rain forest in the United States.

Name _____ Date _____

Vocabulary Activity

Directions: Practice your writing skills. Write at least three sentences using words from the story.

Words from the Story

strike	suddenly	hesitated	creatures
destroyed	tropical	temperate	planet

_____

_____

_____

_____

_____

_____

Directions: Answer this question.

1. Why do you think the man in the story **hesitates** before walking out of the rain forest?

_____

_____

Analyzing the Literature

Provided here are discussion questions you can use in small groups, with the whole class, or for written assignments. Each question is written at two levels so that you can choose the right question for each group of students. For each question, a few key points are provided for your reference as you discuss the book with students.

Story Element	Level 1	Level 2	Key Discussion Points
Character	What does the man decide to do?	In what ways is his decision both easy and hard?	The man decides to leave the forest without cutting down the Kapok tree. He had been given a job to do, but he takes time to consider the message from the animals before deciding to walk away.
Setting	What is the mood of the forest when the man leaves?	What do you think the mood in the forest would have been if the man had continued to chop down the Kapok tree?	The animals in the forest must feel a great sense of relief as the man walks out. If he had decided to cut down the tree, there would have been a sense of helplessness, loss, and desperation.
Plot	What is the message of the story?	What do you think the author wants the readers to do as a result of reading this book?	The purpose of the story is to help people understand what happens when forests are destroyed. The author hopes readers will listen to the messages of the animals and do their part to protect and care for Earth.
Character	What do you like best about the man in this story?	What do you think the man will do after he leaves the rain forest?	The man in the story listens to the animals and decides to save their home. When he leaves, he will have to tell his boss why he did not cut down the Kapok tree. Maybe he will go on to become an advocate for the forest and encourage others to protect the plants and animals of the rain forest.

Name _____ Date _____

Reader Response

Think

The man in this story has to make a difficult decision. Think about difficult decisions you have had to make. What helps you to make those decisions?

Opinion Writing Prompt

The man decides to leave the forest without cutting down the Kapok tree. Do you think he made a good decision? Tell about the decision he made and why you think it was or was not a good decision.

_____

_____

_____

_____

_____

_____

_____

_____

_____

_____

Guided Close Reading

Closely reread the last two pages of the story.

Directions: Think about these questions. In the space below, write ideas or draw pictures as you think. Be ready to share your answers.

❶ Is the decision to leave the forest an easy or hard one for the man? Use the text to support your answer.

❷ What does the man do right before he makes his decision?

❸ Look at the pictures and describe the rain forest.

Name _____ Date _____

Making Connections—Care for Earth

Directions: Lynne Cherry, the author of this book, encourages readers to care for Earth throughout her books. Draw a picture of yourself doing something to help Earth. Make a list of other things you can do to care for our planet.

Things I Can Do to Help Care for Earth

1. _____

2. _____

3. _____

4. _____

5. _____

Language Learning–Synonyms

Directions: Write at least one synonym for each word from the story. You can think of the synonyms on your own or use a dictionary or online resource to help you find synonyms.

Language Hints!

- Synonyms are different words that have the same meaning.

- Synonyms should be the same part of speech.

Word from Story	Synonym
hot The rain forest is **hot**.	*blazing*
leap Animals **leap** from tree to tree.	
quiet It is **quiet** when the men walk into the forest.	
look The snake **looks** at the cut the ax made in the tree.	
disappear The birds are worried that the forest will **disappear**.	
wondrous The plants and animals in the forest are quite **wondrous**.	

Name _____ Date _____

Story Elements–Plot

Directions:

1. Think about your favorite parts of the story.

2. Choose an event from the beginning, the middle, the ending, and one other event of your choice.

3. List each event in the correct sequence in the boxes below.

4. Draw a picture or write about what happens in each event you selected.

Event 1: _____	**Event 2:** _____
Event 3: _____	**Event 4:** _____

Story Elements–Character

Directions: Read the list of animals from the story. Select your favorite animal. Use modeling clay to create your favorite animal. Write a description below of the animal you created.

Materials

• modeling clay in assorted colors

Animals from the Story

boa constrictor	bee	monkeys	toucan
macaw	cock-of-the-rock	tree frog	jaguar
tree porcupines	anteaters	three-toed sloth	

_____

_____

_____

_____

_____

_____

_____

_____

Name _____ Date _____

Post-Reading Theme Thoughts

Directions: Choose a main character from *The Great Kapok Tree*. Pretend you are that character. Draw a picture of a happy face or a sad face to show how the character would feel about each statement. Then use words to explain your picture.

Character I Chose: _____

Statement	How Does the Character Feel? ☺ ☹	What Does the Character Think?
You should follow directions without thinking of the consequences.		
It is all right to cut down a tree in a forest.		
People can change their minds while they sleep.		
One person can make a difference in the world.		

Culminating Activity: Life in a Rain Forest

Directions: Have students read the activity descriptions. Help them choose an activity to complete. Most likely, these activities will require some adult assistance to complete. The pictures on pages 62–64 may be fun for students to use as they prepare their presentations.

- **A Story to Pass Down**—Pretend it is more than 20 years since the story of the Kapok tree took place. Imagine that you are the child who spoke to the man. You are now an adult with children of your own, and you would like to share this experience with them. Write a story to tell your children what you saw and did that day in the rain forest. You may wish to use the pictures on pages 62–64 to help illustrate your story.

- **A Day to Save a Forest**—Through the actions of the animals and the young child, a tree and forest are saved. Write a reader's theater script telling the story of how the forest was saved. Use the pictures on pages 62–64 as you perform your script.

- **A Visit to the Forest**—Create a three-dimensional model of the rain forest. Use craft supplies such as clay, construction paper, leaves, sticks, grass, craft sticks, string, and any other materials that will help make a realistic model of the forest. Use the pictures on pages 62–64 to show what happened in the forest.

Culminating Activity: Life in a Rain Forest *(cont.)*

Directions: Reproduce the images on tagboard or construction paper. You may wish to enlarge pictures for the reader's theater and shrink the pictures for the model activity. Have the students cut out the images along the dashed lines. To create stick puppets, glue each pattern to a tongue depressor or craft stick.

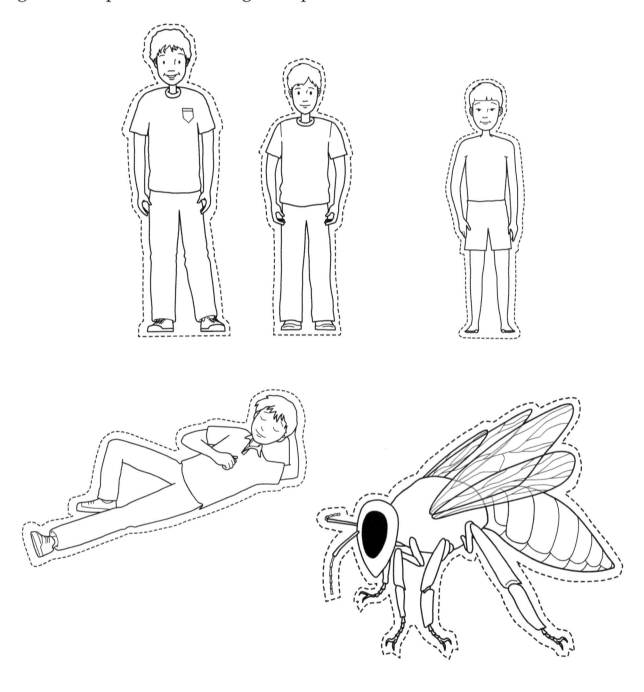

Culminating Activity: Life in a Rain Forest *(cont.)*

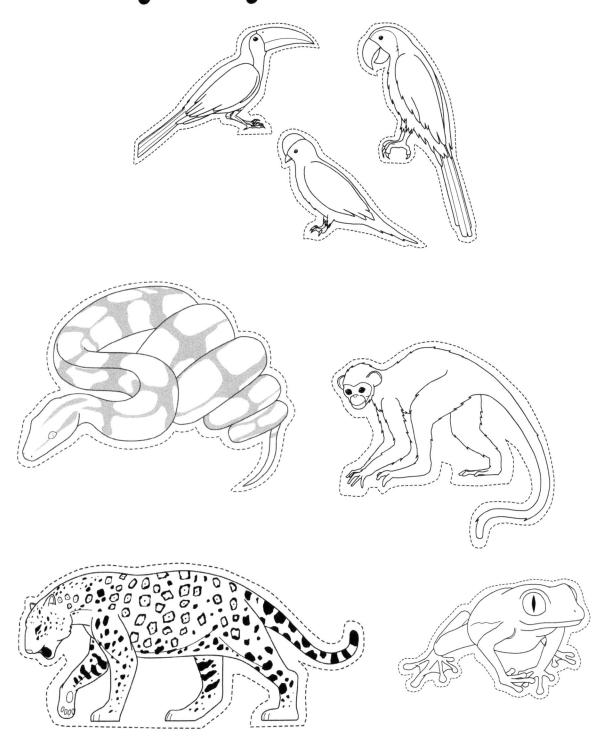

Culminating Activity: Life in a Rain Forest *(cont.)*

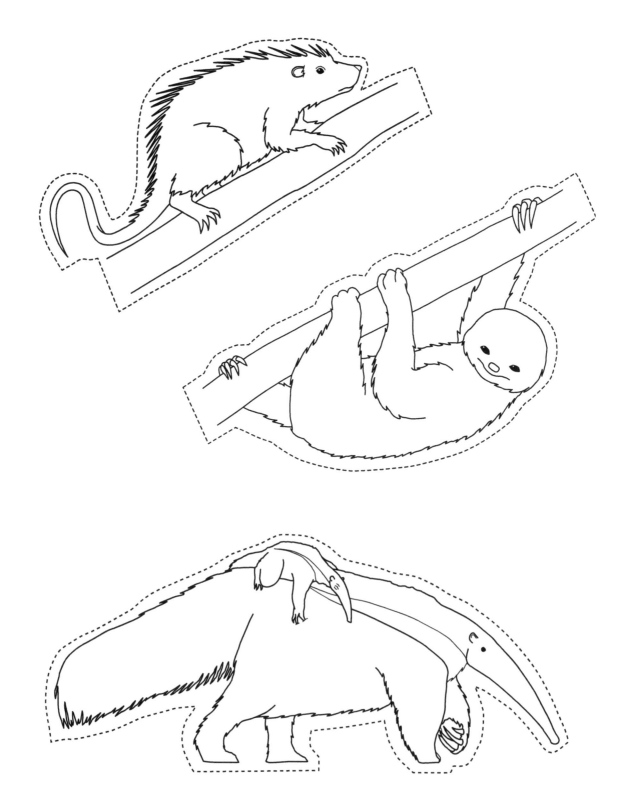

Comprehension Assessment

Directions: Fill in the bubble for the best response to each question.

Entering the Rain Forest

1. What is the problem facing the rain forest?

   (A) Too many people visit the rain forest.

   (B) The homes for plants and animals are being destroyed.

   (C) There is not enough rain for plants to grow.

   (D) Trees are being planted.

Four Groups Visit

2. Which of the following does **not** concern the monkeys?

   (E) The roots of the trees will wither and die.

   (F) There will no longer be beautiful flowers to see.

   (G) The soil will be washed away in the rains, and the forest will become a desert.

   (H) People will continue to come back and take more and more trees.

Five More Groups Visit

3. Which statement best summarizes the concerns of the anteaters?

   (A) When the trees are gone, there will be no oxygen to breathe.

   (B) They will no longer be able to find food to feed their young.

   (C) What people do in the forest today will have consequences in the future.

   (D) There will no longer be a place for the animals to live.

Comprehension Assessment (cont.)

A Child's Visit

4. What does the child mean when he asks the man to look at them with new eyes?

_____

_____

_____

_____

_____

_____

_____

Leaving the Forest

5. What shows that the animals are anxious about the man's decision?

(E) The animals leave before he wakes up.

(F) The animals tell him their homes will be destroyed.

(G) Animals share they will not have food to eat.

(H) The animals are silent as he wakes up.

Response to Literature: Saving the Rain Forest

Directions: Each of the animals presents its reasons for saving the rain forest. Think about which animal's arguments you like best. Draw a picture of that animal talking to the man. In your picture, show the message the animal is presenting to the man. Be sure your picture is neat, detailed, and colorful. Use your drawing to help answer the questions on the next page.

Name _____ Date _____

Response to Literature:
Saving the Rain Forest *(cont.)*

1. Describe what is happening in the rain forest in the scene you drew.

   _____

   _____

   _____

   _____

2. Tell why you like this scene in the rain forest.

   _____

   _____

   _____

   _____

3. What is the message the animal is giving about the importance of the rain forest?

   _____

   _____

   _____

   _____

Name _____ Date _____

Response to Literature Rubric

Directions: Use this rubric to evaluate student responses.

Great Job	Good Work	Keep Trying
☐ You answered all three questions completely. You included many details.	☐ You answered all three questions.	☐ You did not answer all three questions.
☐ Your handwriting is very neat. There are no spelling errors.	☐ Your handwriting can be neater. There are some spelling errors.	☐ Your handwriting is not very neat. There are many spelling errors.
☐ Your picture is neat and fully colored.	☐ Your picture is neat and some of it is colored.	☐ Your picture is not very neat and/or fully colored.
☐ Creativity is clear in both the picture and the writing.	☐ Creativity is clear in either the picture or the writing.	☐ There is not much creativity in either the picture or the writing.

Teacher Comments: _____

_____

_____

_____

Name _____ Date _____

_____

_____

_____

_____

_____

_____

_____

_____

_____

_____

_____

_____

_____

The responses provided here are just examples of what students may answer. Many accurate responses are possible for the questions throughout this unit.

Vocabulary Activity—Section 1:
Entering the Rain Forest (page 16)

- *The Great Kapok Tree* is the story of a **community** of animals that live in a tree.
- **Squawking** and **howling** sounds are made by the birds and monkeys in the forest.
- The great Kapok tree is so tall it **emerges** above the other trees in the forest.
- The **canopy** is a high and sunny place that looks like it touches the sky.
- The heat and sounds of the rain forest **lull** the man to sleep.
1. The **understory** is the lower part of the rain forest. Shrubs, small bushes, shorter trees, ferns, and any other smaller plant life would be seen growing in the understory.

Guided Close Reading—Section 1:
Entering the Rain Forest (page 19)

1. In the preface the words "always hot," "heat," "sunny," and "steamy environment" are used to describe the rain forest. On the second page of text the author tells of the sweat running down the man's face and the heat of the forest.
2. Before the men enter the forest, the animals are making noises. When the men enter, the animals become quiet as they watch and wonder about the men.
3. The larger man points to a tree and leaves the smaller man to cut it down. He seems like the boss.

Vocabulary Activity—Section 2:
Four Groups Visit (page 25)

1. A plant that has been damaged or does not receive enough water or sunlight will **wither** and die.

Guided Close Reading—Section 2:
Four Groups Visit (page 28)

1. The bee explains that it flies from flower to flower to collect pollen. By doing this it pollinates trees and flowers all over the rain forest. The trees and flowers depend on the bee to complete this task that helps them live, grow, and reproduce.
2. The boa constrictor states: "Do not chop it down." The bee explains that the tree is its home and that plants in the forest depend on it. The monkeys explain what will happen if tree after tree is chopped down. The birds tell the man that he "must not cut down this tree."

3. This phrase is open to interpretation. The boa constrictor talks about generations of his family having lived in the tree. He may have memories of things that happened to them. He could also be referring to all the animals that make their home there and all the things they do.

Language Learning—Section 2:
Four Groups Visit (page 30)
Interesting verbs from this section of the story include the following:

- boa constrictor: slithered, slid, hissed
- bee: buzzed, pollinate
- troupe of monkeys: scampered, chattered
- toucan, macaw, cock-of-the-rock: flew, squawked, flown

Vocabulary Activity—Section 3:
Five More Groups Visit (page 34)

- The tree frog tells the man that a **ruined** rain forest means **ruined** lives.
- The jaguar's spotted coat blends into the **dappled** light and shadows of the understory.
- The tree porcupines ask the man if he knows what trees **produce**.
- The anteaters climb down the tree with their babies **clinging** to them.
- The anteater says, "Senhor, you are chopping down this tree with no thought for the **future**."
- The three-toed sloth points out that if the rain forest is destroyed, they won't have anything to **feast their eyes** on.

Guided Close Reading—Section 3:
Five More Groups Visit (page 37)

1. Up until this point, the jaguar was unseen. He pads quietly over to the man and then growls in his ear. The jaguar is concerned that if the tree is cut down, the animals living in it will lose their homes, and the jaguar will have a difficult time finding food to eat.
2. The three-toed sloth sees the beauty in the tree. She is worried that the destruction of the tree will lead to the destruction of the rain forest. If the rain forest is destroyed, there will be nothing beautiful left.
3. The tree frog is concerned that he will be homeless if the Kapok tree is chopped down. The jaguar fears a loss of the birds and animals that he eats. The tree porcupines worry that without trees, less oxygen will be produced.

Answer Key

Language Learning—Section 3:
Five More Groups Visit (page 39)

- A piece of cake—something that is easy
- Hit the books—time to study

Story Elements—Section 3:
Five More Groups Visit (page 41)

1. tree frog—bright, small, squeaky voice, worried about being left homeless
2. jaguar—sleepy, spotted coat, quiet, unhappy, worried about finding food
3. tree porcupines—group of four, quiet, able to swing, worried about oxygen
4. anteaters—have young children, striped and unstriped, able to climb, worried about a world with no trees
5. three-toed sloth—slow, deep and lazy voice, worried about the loss of beauty in the world

Vocabulary Activity—Section 4:
A Child's Visit (page 43)

1. The flowers in the rain forest release a **fragrant** scent.
2. The man realizes that the animals of the forest are **wondrous** and **rare**.
3. The child **murmurs** his request in the man's ear.
4. Sunlight glows like jewels **amidst** the dark colors of the forest.
5. To look at something with new eyes means to see it in a different way. Rather than seeing the forest as a place to be destroyed, the man learns to see the beauty of the plants and animals that live there.

Guided Close Reading—Section 4:
A Child's Visit (page 46)

1. The child seems respectful and cautious as he approaches the sleeping man. The child kneels over the man and murmurs (speaks quietly) in his ear. He uses the word *please* when he asks the man to look at them with new eyes. He is making a request not telling the man what to do.
2. The animals are described as wondrous and rare. These words tell that the animals are unusual, unique, and amazing. The illustrations are detailed showing the color, size, and unique characteristics of each animal.
3. The man sees that the animals are wondrous and rare. He notices the colors in the forest and sees the plants as strange and beautiful. The man also takes time to smell the flowers and feels the mist of the forest floor.

Vocabulary Activity—Section 5:
Leaving the Forest (page 52)

1. The man probably **hesitates** because he might get in trouble with the big man if he doesn't cut down the tree.

Guided Close Reading—Section 5:
Leaving the Forest (page 55)

1. The man stops swinging the ax and looks at the animals and child. He is probably thinking about what they said to him. Then he hesitates before dropping his ax and walks out of the forest. He is likely deciding if it would be best to continue doing his job or to listen to the boy and animals.
2. "Suddenly he stopped." It seems like his decision came upon him without warning.
3. Lush, green plants make up the understory of the rain forest. There are a variety of colorful flowers growing up from the ground and hanging from vines in trees. An assortment of animals both large and small can be seen in the pictures. Some are flying, others are walking on the ground, and others are climbing in vines or trees.

Language Learning—Section 5:
Leaving the Forest (page 57)

Possible synonyms for words are listed:

1. hot—tropical, scorching, very warm, blazing, boiling
2. leap—jump, bound, spring
3. quiet—silent, still, hushed
4. look—view, gaze, glimpse, stare
5. disappear—leave, die out, end, go away
6. wondrous—amazing, magnificent, extraordinary, fascinating

Comprehension Assessment (pages 65–66)

1. B. The homes for plants and animals are being destroyed.
2. F. There will no longer be beautiful flowers to see.
3. C. What people do in the forest today will have consequences in the future.
4. When the young child asks the sleeping man to look at them all with new eyes, he is referring to all the plants and animals around him. The child wants the man to think beyond his job and what he has been told to do. He wants the man to see that there are beautiful, unique plants and animals that make the forest their home. The child wants the man to realize that the decision he makes will have a big impact on all who call the rain forest their home.
5. H. The animals are silent as he wakes up.